Mom and I ride the bicycle to the store or farmers market.
We buy native foods or fresh flowers but especially treats for me!

With my long ears flopping in the wind, we whiz by all the cars and people who wave "hello" to us.

Dedicated to All Dogs
and Their Owners

EL JOFFE

Poodle de Santa Fe

Pamela S. Pease

Quick Facts About Santa Fe

1. Oldest Capital City in North America
2. Founded in 1610 by Spain
3. Over 6000 feet above sea level
4. Famous for Native American Arts and Culture
5. Over 200 Fine Art Galleries
6. World-class Santa Fe Opera House
7. A dog-friendly City for Poodles like me

Get Ready to Meet Joffe
Learn about Santa Fe New Mexico...

First published in 2024
The Euphorion Press Limited

The.euphorion@gmail.com
http://www.theeuphorion.com
Maine, USA

ISBN: 979-8-218-40052-1

Graphic Designer Belinda E. Pease
Papers used by The Euphorion Press are made from wood grown in sustainable forests.

OODLES of POODLES

Did you know?

Poodles are originally from Germany and Russia. They are water dogs, used for hunting and retrieving.

Poodles are "adopted" by France for their high intelligence, bird hunting, loving nature, glamour, and good humor. **Ooh la la!**

Poodles have hair (just like you!), not fur like most dogs. Therefore, they do not shed their hair or make you sneeze.

Poodles love to jump and play, using their two front paws as arms, and love to 'smile' too!

Poodles are adored on "Poodle Skirts". These favorite skirts are liked by younger girls, as they are made with a "glittery poodle" on the front and shaped in a circle for spinning around and around.

Poodles are sensitive, gentle, curious and love children.

Poodles are considered to be human-like in their intelligence. Experts cite Poodles as the smartest among all dogs.

Poodles are bred in 4 sizes: toy, miniature, standard and royal. **(Joffe is a Standard size at 21 kilos or 46 pounds.)**

Poodles are white, black **(that's me!)**, brown, apricot, party poodles (black and white), and silver.

Poodles are winners in the famous USA Westminster Dog Show. Siba, a black Standard Poodle, won BEST IN SHOW in 2020.

Poodles in the United States are recognized and registered by the American Kennel Club (AKC).

EL Joffe has AKC registration, required for competition in The Westminster Dog competition.

♦♦♦

Oodles of Poodles come out to play,

Frisking and leaping till the end of the day,

When all is quiet,

They snuggle together,

Ready for the night!

– EL Joffe

EL JOFFE

Joffe is a POODLE. ***A beautiful poodle.***

Joffe means "BEAUTIFUL" in the Hebrew language. Even the famous Dr. Sigmund Freud named his loving dog companion "Joffe". That is why I am called Joffe!

I am covered with fluffy soft hair (not fur!) so no one will sneeze!

I was born on a farm in Durango, Colorado.

My two pedigree-poodle parents are both members of the American Kennel Club (AKC).

My handsome Doggie Dad is “Romeo” and *beautiful Mom is “Juliet”.*

Together Romeo and Juliet had 10 beautiful and colorful puppies. Some were apricot, some white, some silver and a couple like me were as black as night!

Hello, my name is Joffe, and I have a lot to tell you.

Firstly, I am the smallest of 10 puppies.

People called me the “runt of the litter”.

Secondly, I am so peppy and bright, my human parents adopted me right away.

It was love at first sight!

I started out being the size of a small book, but within a year when you looked at me, I stood tall and weighed 46 pounds (21 kilos).

No matter my size, I always love to be cuddled in my Dad's lap... they called me a **'sweet lap dog'**!

My real adventures started when the three of us settled together in **"The City Different" — SANTA FE**, New Mexico!

Like my parents, I love Santa Fe for its history, art, music, beautiful winding narrow streets...plus, an abundance of wonderful Poodle friends everywhere!

I know
I can find a
bestie friend here
to play with!
Somewhere!

For me, I want to understand everything about Santa Fe.

As a POODLE growing up in the "high desert", every day seems different with all the music, art and culture offered in Santa Fe!

The beautiful desert landscape with vast turquoise skies and deep purple and red sunsets are magical.

This is why the State of New Mexico is called the **"Land of Enchantment"**.

Imagine this fact! The mountains are over 12,000 feet high (or 4000 meters)...so, there is less air than at sea-level! Wow, my breathing changes when I walk and run...who would have guessed that my lungs are getting stronger and stronger!

I find Santa Fe *different* and enchanting in my quest to find a “bestie” friend!

The Native Americans have a special relationship with the land, which they share with us in their arts and culture. After all, there are more than 8 ***different*** Native American Reservations near Santa Fe. They love dogs, too.

They are very talented: spiritual dancing, painting, world-class jewelry of silver and turquoise, and pottery made from the local clay earth.

For example...my Dad has a Bolo Tie, my Mom a Concho Belt as well as a Squash Necklace. The Squash Necklace is my favorite as it shows off my black hair!

I love seeing their traditional jewelry, especially when they perform Buffalo Dancing in the City's Plaza! Their skilled drumming and dancing always puts a smile on my face.

My parents know I love music and dancing. It makes me feel wild and free, like a puppy again!

Other doggies watching me just roll their eyes! ***But I don't care.***

Santa Fe means "Holy Faith"

Amazingly, settlers from Spain founded the City in 1610.

The Spanish called the City, **La Villa Real de la Santa Fe de San Francisco de Asís** (meaning: "The Royal City of the Holy Faith of Saint Francis of Assisi").

Saint Francis is the lover of all animals such as birds, rabbits, dogs, and lambs. He continues to be worshipped with many statues, as well as small tin tags in his image, which can be purchased around the City. There are many stories of his extraordinary kindness to animals.

Thought I might find a bestie friend hanging out nearby!

Spanish traditions are still alive in Santa Fe and make for a different culture. Sometimes, I feel like I am in Spain rather than the USA.

My parents often speak in both Spanish and English to me — just like they do in other countries.

Many people here understand and speak both languages, sometimes at the same time.

It makes me feel dizzy in the head!!

Santa Fe is *different* since it is not only the oldest Capital City in the United States, but also the oldest Capital City in North America.

It is located in the Southwestern State of New Mexico.

New Mexico is surrounded by the States of Colorado (where I was born) to the NORTH, Arizona to the WEST, and Texas to the EAST. Below New Mexico, in the SOUTH, lies the separate country of Mexico.

Humm, my parents have friends who moved from Texas, they have a handsome white French Bulldog — ooh la la! ***Could he be my best friend? He lives near me and his name is Phil!***

Believe it or not, some people, even in the United States, think New Mexico is a different country — and not a State within the USA!

This is very funny for me!

More Stones than Grass

For Poodles and for my new friend Phil, there is virtually no green grass to play or pee on!

I grew up knowing only dirt roads and a yard full of beautiful stones laid out, as far as I can see and run.

ZIA Symbol

Four is a sacred number for Zia Native Americans. The circle with its four rays stretching outwards each representing one of the four seasons: spring, summer, autumn and winter.

How ***different*** is it to have this ancient image of the SUN on the **State Flag** — the "**Sun Sign**"? Yes it is true, we have nearly 320 days of sunshine per year!

State Bird

Even more special but ***different***, the State Bird is the Roadrunner!

Lucky me, I have **Roadrunners** living outside my front door.

I run and run trying to catch them, but they are faster than a mouse!

Famous Santa Fe Trail

Have you ever heard of the United States (US) Route 66?

This major highway runs through many cities in the Southwestern USA.

However, it is ***different*** in Santa Fe. The old US Route 66 connects with the famous "Santa Fe Trail" — which runs through the City Center called "The Plaza"!

Adobe Homes

Our house is built ***differently*** from other modern houses! It is more like a house in Old Spain but only located in the USA.

Santa Feans use a mixture of clay and straw dried in the sun to form bricks. These bricks are called Adobe. Therefore, the mud-brick homes along with their flat roofs are called **Adobe homes**.

This type of house is so special that it is also known as ***Santa Fe Style***.

My house is Santa Fe Style.

It has a flat roof with a viewing deck on top.

I can actually walk on the roof and invite my friends over for a hoot or to play.

How many Poodles can say that? ***Oodles of Poodles!***

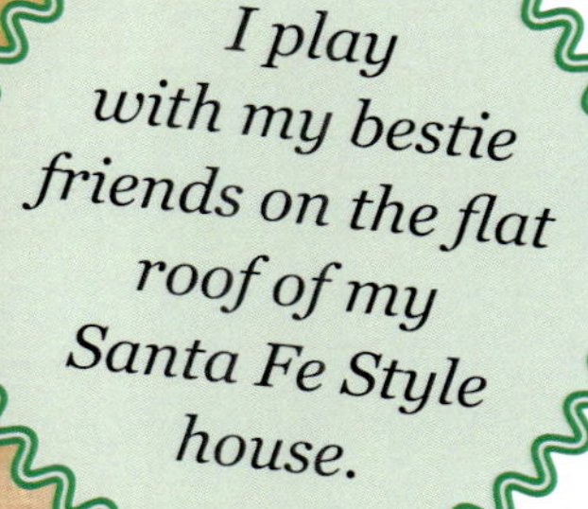

My parents often gaze at the beautiful high mountains surrounding us or else they **view one of our red sunsets in the distance.**

This is a delight! Being a "lap dog", I often jump up to be cuddled while the sun sets in the West.

No question about it! My house is Santa Fe Style. An adobe house made from the red clay earth formed into large mud bricks, dried in our hot, summer sun. The walls are more than 12 inches (30 cm) thick. This keeps the house cool in the midsummer heat, and warm during the cool winters.

My house has accents of handcrafted wood doors and beams like many Spanish buildings, too!

Also, I love our round fireplaces called "**kivas**". We have three of them! Who wouldn't find Santa Fe Style enchanting!

Flat Roof and Colors from Nature

My parents told me that all the houses in the City of Santa Fe are required to look more like nature so they blend into the landscape. **This is very *different*.**

That is why they are painted in brown or red colors — just like the colors of the earth — dirt and stones I pee on.

Hee Hee!

There are no tall buildings, as far as I can see. Just short **Pinon Pine Trees**, which grow pine nuts for eating and cooking. Also, juniper shrubs and clumps of yellow flowering **Chamisa**, everyone calls "Rabbit Bushes" because big "Jack Rabbits" can hide in them.

Sunny Days, Dry Air and Fluffy Snow

Imagine over 320 sunny days out of 360 days a year? The weather of Santa Fe is very ***different*** due its height. I use the word "***different***" a lot, don't I!

I live one and half miles (or 2.4 Kilometers) higher than the ocean. Some days, I feel like I can reach the sun with my nose by standing on our flat roof top.

But did you also know? The air is very dry for most of the year. However, it sometimes snows in the winter months.

If I travel to the top of the largest mountain above us, I could go skiing when it snows. I dream about skiing and one day I will do it!

So, I love to experience the beauty of the white snow set against the brown adobe houses and mountains. When the sun comes out in winter the snow melts quickly. **Do you know why? Ha — because we are higher!**

Even the metal Statue in our garden is beautiful with snow clinging to it, like frosting on a cake. My Mom even put a big red necktie on it for decoration!

After a snow fall, I kick up my heels and run and play in the snow. My parents say I am ***"frisky in the snow"***.

All my friends, including Phil, come out to play too. Everyone is 'frisky'.

With my nose disappearing into the fresh snow, I feel like I am going for a swim in the sea — wet and wild for all of us!!!

**I love my life in Santa Fe.
Every day brings fresh new adventures!**

My morning job

I have a lot of energy. So, I always dream of having a job like my parents.

When I was six months old, my parents taught me how to run out the front door, up the red brick driveway to grab the morning newspaper. I then bring it home for all to read.

It's my job and I do it very well!

It puts a big smile on my parents faces because they think it is swell!

I am proud my job helps my family!

Not only that, but there is also a reward... cuddling in the lap of my Mom or Dad! They adore me, I can see it in their eyes... as I love them too!

THEN comes breakfast before my morning walk!

I love walking in Santa Fe near my house or through the City Plaza. It's fun to see my doggy friends (especially Phil!) as well as my human friends!!

These walks are full of adventures, some gleeful but sometimes spine-shivering!

These walks are sometimes full of scary surprises!

What has a spade-shaped face, scales shaped like a diamond on its skin, and slithers when it moves? A **"Diamond Back Rattlesnake"**, you might say, and you are right! These markings make them easy to identify.

In the summer, Rattlesnakes lie in the middle of the road to soak up the heat from the sun! Oh, they love Santa Fe's dry hot weather, hiding in scrubby bushes, or amid the rocks. I see them when I go walking.

If their tail is pointed upward toward the sky and shaking, it sounds like a "rattle", and this is a warning. ***Don't come any closer!***

One cold day in November, my Mom and I were stalked by a Mountain Lion — also called a Cougar!

The day was very cold and snowy. Neither cars nor people were around. We were all alone in the early, cool morning.

The hungry **Cougar** spotted us immediately. He probably hadn't eaten for days and now... **Lunch had arrived**! He started following us!

I heard him walking as clear as a bell, crushing snow under his paws as he went. My hearing is very acute and better than most humans. I believe he was after me, as I was just a puppy then. Good for a snack.

When I pulled on my leash, my Mom turned and saw the Cougar very near us. She saved us from being attacked by jumping up on a rock wall and waving her arms wildly in the air. Doing this made her look very big — bigger than life! Finally, the Cougar ran away, and we were saved.

I think my Mom was scared too, as we ran home together as fast as a bolt of lightning! Scary, but also another adventure!

Have you ever heard of "Wily Coyote" who lives in the hills around my house?

Looks like a dog only it howls instead of barking! "Wild" as the wind! Sneaky like a Mountain Lion.

When I see a coyote in my yard or on the street, I stop and find protection as quickly as possible. They look like me and are smart. However, they are known to attack my other doggy friends — including big Poodles and even my new friend Phil!

Two coyotes once surrounded my Mom and I. We were walking to the City Plaza down the road from our adobe house. One coyote came up to grab my tail, while another one was in front of my Mom. I am a gentle dog who never attacks anyone.

An "easy peasey" meal for them!

We grabbed a big stick to protect us should they come closer.

Lucky for us — just in the nick of time — my Dad drove by in his car. He saw us surrounded and quickly steered the car straight at the coyotes — scaring them away.

Then we jumped into the car to be safe and secure with Dad!

Phew, that was a close call!

Nevertheless, most of my days and walks are very fun adventures!

Mom and I ride the bicycle to the store or farmers market. We buy native foods or fresh flowers but especially treats for me!

With my long ears flopping in the wind, we whiz by all the cars and people who wave "hello" to us.

I really like our outings to the Santa Fe Farmers Market on Saturday mornings! Often, I see Phil with his Mom and Dad, too!

All of us together have treats, coffee, listen to music, mingle with friends, and buy locally farmed or baked foods!

In September, the famous green chiles are roasted for us to buy directly from the farmers. Then, we make my favorite dish: spicy hot, Santa Fe chile stew!

We all have fun, watching the roasting over the hot fire...as the green chiles slowly but surely turn brown!

Other people love just air-drying red chiles for weeks. Then, they string them together and hang them on buildings for colorful decoration in the Fall and during the Christmas holidays. They are called Ristras.

Once a month, I go to the grooming salon. Poodles have hair instead of fur. I need it cut and styled. Ha! Just like humans — like my Mom and Dad.

My Dad drops me off on his way to work. I spend the day at the Spa, playing with my human and doggy friends, all the while having my luxury haircut! There are plenty of treats and cuddles too!

The next day, I am so happy to visit the art galleries, showing off my new groovy, hip style! ***Ooh la la!***

My parents told me that Santa Fe is an ‘art lovers dream’! There are more than 250 galleries full of first-class art. Santa Fe is recognized world-wide by UNESCO (United Nations Educational, Scientific and Cultural Organization) as a ‘Creative City’ — a hub of art creation.

I love artists (including of course my Mom), as many of them in Santa Fe have Poodles like me. Oh, Phil’s Mom is a writer and poet-artist in her own right!

My favorite walk is through the 50 or more galleries on Canyon Road, a famous street full of art. I always see the creative, colorful paintings and their artists, but best of all there are the **Oodles of Poodles!**

Even the gallery owners, give me treats for being very polite and nice — no barking and jumping!

Mom and I walk twice a week along Canyon Road, sometimes we even have coffee (and treats) at an "art lovers" cafe!

We are so lucky to have this beauty around us!

Many famous artists make Santa Fe their home.

One of my favorite artists is Georgia O'Keeffe.
She lived in the wild desert with only her dog to keep her company. What a pioneer she was, moving to Santa Fe from New York City long ago…1929!

Mom and I view her paintings at the "Georgia O'Keeffe Museum" in the City Center. I stand there on my four paws, alongside my Mom admiring the art.

Just like me, Georgia learned about the unique colors of Santa Fe. She painted the turquoise sky, red earth, yellow desert flowers, and brown shapes — all the jagged and eroded hill sides.

Maybe you too have seen Georgia O'Keeffe's art?

My favorite paintings include her use of common symbols such as the a **head of a fearsome bull along with bird feathers and flowers everywhere.**

Wowser, I get excited about all types of art including paintings of course, but also weaving, pottery, and sculpture.

I love visiting the adobe galleries with art inside and outside for all to see — Santa Fe Style. It's as if the buildings blend into Nature.

Do you know "sculpture"? Can you find the coyote-man, arms outstretched, holding his totem?

After all, Poodles love art...***can you find me too?***

Talking about art! My Mom often takes me to her Art Group once a week.

They are all wonderful artists, painting and talking. Mom even painted the pictures for my book. I just love being included in these gatherings!

The best is when they go to lunch. I am always invited as even the nicest restaurants allow poodles!

The other day, my Mom painted this picture of me. I just love it! I look very edgy on my favorite spiky rug.

Guess what I now know?
My parents go to the Santa Fe Opera, Symphony and Indian Art Exhibitions throughout the summer — June to September.

But the best thing for me is the live music and dancing at the Plaza — City Center. ***It is relaxing and joyous community event for doggy and human friends!***

The concerts are free to all residents and visitors, and doggie friends too!

Every week in the summer, there is a different band playing in the Plaza Bandstand. Music includes rock'n roll bands, hip-hop, jazz, country blues or even opera singers!

Mom, Dad and I bring a picnic basket full of food to eat as we sit listening to the music! We wear our best turquoise jewelry, and dancing shoes! **We dance for a long time, smiling all the while!**

It's a real hoot!

Let me tell you about my favorite event!

The **Annual Pet Parade** marks the end of Summer! It's also the beginning of the **Spanish Fiesta de Santa Fe** celebration. It makes me believe Saint Francis' love of animals is alive and celebrated!

The **Pet Parade** event is just for pets and their families! My friend Phil and his parents go to this too!

Santa Fe dogs, cats, turtles, birds, snakes, rabbits and goats all participate by dressing up in costumes. I dress up too, and march with the music throughout the City Center.

Treats and candy are tossed out into the street for pets and children. *This is the sweetest event of the year for me!* ***HA! HA!***

I look forward to the cooler Fall days. My Mom and Dad invite friends to our house for Santa Fe Chili Stew with cornbread or tortillas.

Our kiva (round) fireplace burns with the sweet smell of Pinion Pine. The best part is that Phil, the French Bull Dog, my bestie doggy friend gets to come over! We play together, tugging and pulling, while our parents have a happy time!

Oh...life is such an enchanting gift for a Santa Fe Poodle living and sleeping in front of my fireplace with snow on the mountain tops.

I find the Holiday Season very special, when the snow falls. It's December and Santa Fe is alight with decorations and musical celebrations.

Farolitos ("little fires") are everywhere: tiny burning candles are placed inside brown paper bags shaped like lanterns.

We use them to celebrate the Holidays — Christmas, Hanukkah, and Kwanzaa.

The lights of the Farolitos are bright!
Yes, hundreds of farolitos are placed along pathways, buildings and local houses — my home too!

On Christmas Eve, we celebrate the Holidays by walking with Phil, my doggie bestie, along Canyon Road with our friends.

A Spanish tradition is lighting Farolitos along all the buildings on Canyon Road's street of galleries. No cars are allowed — only dogs and people!

Bonfires are ablaze in the center of the street. Art galleries celebrate by serving free hot drinks and Spanish cookies for people. Meanwhile, doggie friends are served peanut butter treats.

Oodles of Poodles come out to celebrate, too.

I love getting into my own bed. I am tired after a full year of adventures and learning about Santa Fe!

Some nights, I just curl up in a ball and dream about everything I've seen. As a Poodle I am very intelligent and love to learn new things, but you probably know this by now!

Falling asleep, I often imagine a **Kokopelli**. Kokopelli is the magical flute player, spreading joy and goodwill, much loved by Native Americans — displayed in homes and adobe buildings across Santa Fe.

Ah, dreams I have...Kokopelli makes me happy, drumming and dancing, spreading the joy of life. I dream of my bestie friend Phil and I playing together in my courtyard!

Life is divine and enchanting for EL JOFFE — *Poodle de Santa Fe!*

Oodles of Poodles come out to play,

Frisking and leaping till the end of the day,

When all is quiet,

They snuggle together,

Ready for the night!

Good Night or Buenas Noches, as we say here!

To all my new friends...El Joffe

El Joffe is a “globe-trotting” Poodle traveling in the United States, France, Spain, and even Australia.

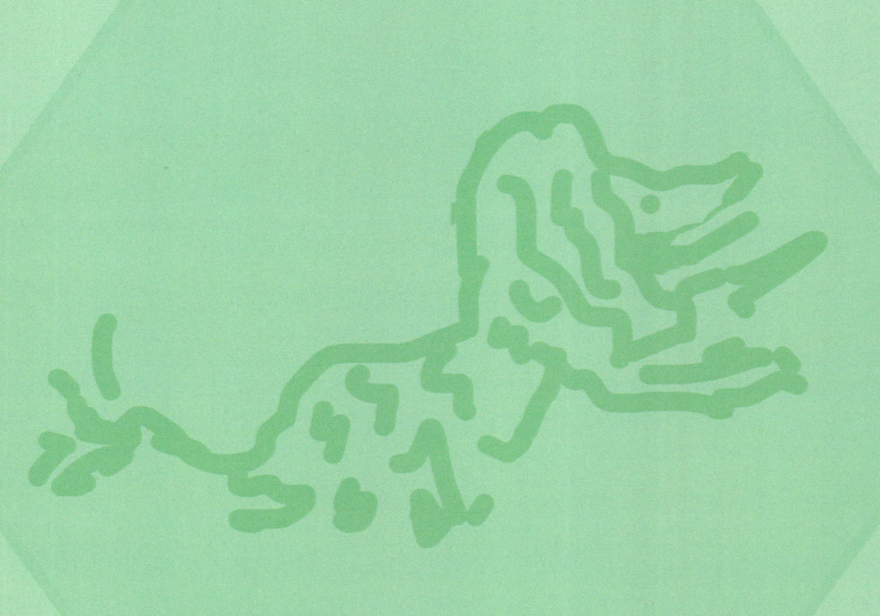

Pamela S. Pease, PhD has lived for over 20 years in Santa Fe, New Mexico USA with her husband and beautiful Joffe. She mastered drawing and painting in the dog-centric, world class art community of "The City Different". Creativity has guided her professionally, as a pioneer implementing new media in education — holding a PhD and Master's degrees. Like Joffe, she has been globe trotting — living in Australia, France, and Italy too.